# BASKETBALL:
# *FORWARD*

by Christina Earley

T0008917

A Stingray Book

## SEAHORSE
### PUBLISHING

# Teaching Tips for Caregivers and Teachers:

This Hi-Lo book features high-interest subject matter that will appeal to all readers in intermediate and middle school grades. It may be enjoyed by students reading at or above grade level as well as by those who are looking for age-appropriate themes matched with a less challenging reading level. Hi-Lo books are ideal for ELL readers, too.

Each book appeals to a striving reader's age and maturity level. Opportunities are provided for students to read words they already know while encountering a limited number of new, high-interest vocabulary words. With these supports in place, students will read more fluently while increasing reading comprehension. Use the following suggestions to help students grow as readers.

- Encourage the student to read independently at home.
- Encourage the student to practice reading aloud.
- Encourage activities that require reading.
- Establish a regular reading time.
- Have the student write questions about what they read.

# Teaching Tips for Teachers:

## Before Reading

- Ask, "What do I know about this topic?"
- Ask, "What do I want to learn about this topic?"

## During Reading

- Ask, "What is the author trying to teach me?"
- Ask, "How is this like something I already know?"

## After Reading

- Discuss how the text features (headings, index, etc.) help with understanding the topic.
- Ask, "What interesting or fun fact did you learn?"

# TABLE OF CONTENTS

# WHAT IS A FORWARD?

Forward is a position on a basketball team.

There are small forwards and power forwards.

They both get **rebounds**.

Sometimes, they score points.

jersey

shorts

shoes

# UNIFORM

All players wear a jersey, or shirt, without sleeves.

Loose-fitting shorts complete the bottom of the uniform.

Uniforms are made of special material that dries fast and stays cool.

Shoes have a **canvas** upper with a rubber sole.

## FUN FACT

Michael Jordan had to pay fines for wearing his famous shoes since they used to be against the NBA dress code.

Forwards practice different **drills** on the court.

They exercise to build **stamina**.

Eating healthy food and drinking water give the energy needed for a game.

## FUN FACT

LeBron James was 18 years 334 days old when he was the youngest player in the NBA to score 30+ points in a game.

# DURING THE GAME

Forwards fight for rebounds close to the basket.

They block shots.

Small forwards make outside shots.

They will take on the best scorer on the **opposing** team.

# TYPES OF FORWARDS

Small forwards are playmakers and defenders.

They make outside shots and get rebounds.

Power forwards play close to the basket.

Their main skill is rebounding.

## FUN FACT

Some of the greatest players in the NBA were small forwards.

# HISTORY

In 1891, James Naismith had to create an indoor activity that could be played by college students in the winter.

Peach baskets were the nets.

Part of the 13 original rules explained the positions.

One of the positions was named the forward.

## FUN FACT

Each time a player made a basket, the referee would have to get the ball out of the peach basket since there was no hole for it to drop through.

# TRAITS OF A GOOD FORWARD

Forwards are excellent with rebounding.

They know how to **muscle** their way in for a position under the basket.

**Blocking** shots is an important skill for being a forward.

# NOTES FROM THE COACH

- Be a leader on and off the court.

- Listen and take constructive criticism from coaches and teammates.

- Admit mistakes and improve.

- Have **grit** to never give up even when things are tough.

- Learn all parts of the game and all positions.

- Work hard during practices and in games.

- Eat a well-balanced diet.

- Have a good attitude and be respectful to others.

### CHARLES BARKLEY

College: Auburn University
- NBA MVP 1992
- Played in 11 All-Star games
- Five-time All-NBA First Team

### LARRY BIRD

College: Indiana State University
- NBA champion 1981, 1984, 1986
- NBA MVP 1983, 1984, 1985
- Played in 12 All-Star games

### TAMIKA CATCHINGS

College: University of Tennessee
- WNBA MVP 2011
- Ten-time All-Star
- Seven-time All-WNBA First Team

### TIM DUNCAN

College: Wake Forest University
- Played in 15 All-Star games
- NBA champion 1999, 2003, 2005, 2007, 2014
- NBA MVP 2001, 2002

### KEVIN DURANT

College: University of Texas Austin
- NBA MVP 2013
- NBA champion 2017, 2018
- Four-time NBA scoring champion 2010, 2011, 2012, 2014

## JULIUS ERVING

College: University of Massachusetts
- ABA champion 1974, 1976; NBA champion 1983
- Played in 16 All-Star games
- ABA MVP 1973, 1974, 1975; NBA MVP 1980

## LEBRON JAMES

High School: Saint Vincent-Saint Mary, Akron, Ohio
- NBA MVP 2008, 2009, 2011, 2012
- NBA champion 2012, 2013, 2016, 2020
- Played in 17 All-Star games

## KARL MALONE

College: Louisiana Tech University
- Played in 14 All-Star games
- NBA MVP 1996, 1998
- All-NBA First Team 11 times

## MAYA MOORE

College: University of Connecticut
- WNBA MVP 2014
- Played in six All-Star games
- Five-time All-WNBA First Team

## DIRK NOWITZKI

High School: Röntgen, Würzburg, Germany
- NBA champion 2011
- NBA MVP 2006
- Played in 14 All-Star games

# GLOSSARY

**blocking** (BLOK·ing): legally deflecting a field goal attempt

**canvas** (KAN·vuhs): a strong, coarse, unbleached cloth

**drills** (drilz): exercises for practicing skills

**grit** (grit): courage and strength of character

**muscle** (MUHS·uhl): to use physical strength to force your way in or to move past

**opposing** (uh·POH·zing): playing against or in competition with

**rebounds** (REE·bownds): acts of gaining possession of a basketball after it has rebounded, or bounced back after a missed shot

**stamina** (STAM·uh·nuh): the ability to sustain prolonged physical or mental effort

# INDEX

# AFTER READING QUESTIONS

1. What does the special material in a basketball uniform do?

2. What is a forward's main skill?

3. What were the nets in the first-ever basketball game?

# About the Author

Christina Earley lives in sunny Florida with her husband and son. She has always loved different sports. She enjoys traveling to see different stadiums, arenas, and ballparks where she always has to eat the local hot dog.

Written by: Christina Earley
Design by: Kathy Walsh
Editor: Kim Thompson

Photographs/Shutterstock: Cover, Pg 1, 5©OSTILL is Franck Camhi, Cover, P 3-22 ©ExpressVectors: Cover Pg 5, 6, 9, 10, 11, 14, 17, 18 ©Oleksii Sidorov: Pg 5 ©Photo Works: Pg 6 ©@Wiki: Pg 9 ©@Wiki: Pg 10©Debby Wong: Pg 13 ©Mark Fann: Pg 14 ©@Wiki: Pg 17 Photo Works: Pg 18 ©Photo Works: Pg 23 ©Debby Wong

**Library of Congress PCN Data**
Basketball: Forward / Christina Earley
 Sports Positions
 ISBN 978-1-63897-107-8 (hard cover)
 ISBN 978-1-63897-193-1 (paperback)
 ISBN 978-1-63897-279-2 (EPUB)
 ISBN 978-1-63897-365-2 (eBook)
Library of Congress Control Number: 2021945200

Printed in the United States of America.

## Seahorse Publishing Company

www.seahorsepub.com

**Published in the United States**
**Seahorse Publishing**
PO Box 771325
Coral Springs, FL 33077